Poetic Moments

by Vera deCicco

Poetic Moments

Copyright © 2015 by Vera deCicco

ISBN-13: 978-0692484920
ISBN-10: 0692484922

Dunton Publishing
New York, New York
www.duntonpublishing.com

Dedication

This volume of poems is dedicated to my beloved brother Joel. Having entered the heavenly realm ten years ago, he is still present in moments of laughter, light-heartedness; small and big stuff alike.

To Joel, who taught me how to nourish and care for others, giving true compassion beyond measure. Miss you bro...

Acknowledgments

I am pleased to acknowledge many of my friends and family for supporting and encouraging me to continue to write poetry as an expression of creativity and spirituality. It is truly a labor of love.

I acknowledge the Holy Spirit as the true author and finisher of this work.

Forward

In passing through, I say to you
Keep it light and keep it moving.

Description

These poems came out of a series of emails called "Poem of the Week," which later transitioned into *Poetic Moments*.

During rather uneven times in my life poetry seems the best way to address the human condition, with all of its turmoil and absurdity. Perhaps a poem can speak volumes to the heart when the head is stuck in the mire of materiality. And so it goes, and so it goes, we grow in ways we know not of.

Table of Contents

Poetic Moments

Peek a Boo

Peek a boo
I see you
vegging out
on the couch
what a place
to find your pace
and stop the race
running here and
running there
has worn you out
relax not collapse
ebb and flow
pause the go.

Stirrings

stirrings
stirred up
stir fry
stir crazy
stirring the soup
stir the air
stir the water
stir the earth
stir the fire
deep deep stirrings
of the earth
the cosmic mama
stirring stirring
to greet the dawn
to settle the day
stirrings
whisper loudly

cosmic mama
puts it politely
stop stirring
the balance
of nature
what the frack do we know
and still we stir.

Vera deCicco

Star Lights

the heavens
are aglow
life streams
above and
below
how do
stars know
when a light
is dimmed
stillness fills
the sky
rocks cry out
trees weep
earth moans
stars know.

Resurfacing

after much to do
too much to do
resurfacing
coming up to the
top again
returning from
some deep sea diving
in the pool of uncertainty
was it a cold
was it the flu
or just too much to do
the world is still with us
and we are still in the world
some subtle adjustments
and wow
my metro card demagnetized
again

Vera deCicco

checks lost in the mail
suddenly reappeared
the android updates
rearranged themselves
into something
from another
planet
and so it goes
and so it goes
resurfacing.

Coordinates

does her hat
match her gloves
do her gloves
match her sox
coordinates
look closely
does her smile
match her mood
most importantly
do her thoughts
match her words
coordinates
time to reassess
no matching sets
just a big mess
bless the mess
move on uncoordinated.

Vera deCicco

Concurrent Realities

concurrent
city memories
the new New York
over layers
the NYC
I once knew
and walked
through
the new New York
replaces
places
once known
by many
seen now by some
as memories
recalled
in an old movie

so strange
and unfamiliar
Times Square
Columbus Circle
Chelsea
Chinatown
the skyline
uneven
jaggered
the old NYC
lies just
beneath
the
concurrent
layers of concrete
along Broadway.

Manhattan

in the middle of
Manhattan
here inside
this modern
over grown
hustling place
the sky is getting
smaller and smaller
the buildings getting
taller and taller
the streets
stranger and stranger
the stores
richer and richer
around the edges
outside of this town
light
can be found.

The World Inside My Phone

this tiny
window
shows me
all
the info
that
I need
to know
hot news
email blues
facebook
twitter
down the
rabbit hole
I go
into a
world of
fractured distraction.

25

Vera deCicco

Belongings

belongings
as in
bits and pieces
of a scattered
life
belongings
as in
heart felt
longings
for a lost
loved one
belongings
as in
please take
all of your

personal
belongings
with you
as you leave
the train.

Sameness

similarities
familiarities
sameness
we seek
sameness
as a
validation
of identity
as if
history
replicates
itself
thru you
and me.

Sanctity

*the sanctity
of the subway
an inner
sanctum
no cell phone
just my
own device
self contained
cerebral
socially
inner active
transportation.*

The Vacation

going where
from where
what is there
when you get there
clean air
beware
you are
there
the you
that
comes and goes
and never knows
the vacation.

Families

families
begin
to fade
when one
head member
dissolves
into
the light
shortly
after
another
follows
or
a new babe
is born
families
rearrange

themselves
upon
the merging
of a marriage
relocation
separation
disassociation
new bonds
form from
the most
unlikely
places
co workers
traveling
companions
families

form from
neighbors
strangers
in passing
or spiritual
pods
familiar
friends
group
together and
families form into
ONE.

6 Cents

there is
6 cents
on my
metrocard
how far
will we
go on
6 cents
think about it
sixth sense
we will
go far
with a
sixth sense
as far as
the stars
and back again
6 cents.

Duct Tape

it seems
these days
my life
is held
together
with
duct tape
the loose
ends
stick together
better
with
duct tape
the checkbook
the hospital visits
the subway rides
the chaos
the heat

Vera deCicco

the medical reports
somehow
sliding away
all day
but for the
duct tape.

Rent Stabilized

(or false security)
rent stabilized
in a changing world
of uncertainty
and
harshness
I am
rent stabilized
the environment weeps
politics shatter
entire economies
collapse
countries
dissolve
in the midst
of it all
I am rent stabilized

generations march on
space travel
progresses
the earth
changes orbit
still
I am rent stabilized
religions
revolve
relationships
collide
what care I
in the midst
of it all
rent stabilized
am I.

Cellophane Noodles

my life is
see through
as in
cellophane noodles
instant visibility
open
revealed
seen
by all
who care
to see
cellophane
noodles.

Ebb and Flow

We get to know
there is
an ebb and flow
a push and pull
a start and stop
a go and come
to all of life's
balance.

Is There a Unicorn in the Living Room?

is there a unicorn
in the living room
makes one
stop and wonder
is there something
I forgot to do
or say or finish
is there a unicorn
in the living room
perhaps it was the IRS
or the many broken agreements
or the
unwrapped wounds
still the thought
haunts me
is there a unicorn in the room
have you looked lately?

Vera deCicco

Branching Out

in faith
with strength
you are
branching out
just as a
tree grows
you are
branching out
trees remain
rooted and grounded
while at the same time
trees are branching out
remember your roots
while growing and
expanding
and branching out.

Late Afternoon

in late afternoon
of life am I
almost evening
not quite
afternoon either
late afternoon
when day is
turning into
night and
glimpses
of
light still prevail
twilight
when the late
evening becomes
midnight
life seems

Vera deCicco

to fade
into another
phase
and disappear
dawn strikes
life begins anew.

After the Storm

the mass transit system
is down in my hometown
the world outside
my window has
shifted from
the known
to the unknown
life as we once lived it
is now dramatically
unraveled
time to get resourceful
and bend with the wind
letting go
is a choice
after the storm.

Spiritual Refugee

everyone is a spiritual
refugee in one form
or another
running here and there
to catch a glimpse
of GOD
searching and seeking
only to find
we left GOD
behind
somewhere between
Nepal and Santa Fe
could it be
GOD lives in me
no longer a spiritual
refugee.

Fast forward

life is streaming by
at an alarming pace
with all kinds of
gadgets in your face
fast forward as we race
what's the hurry
when we get there
what's the use
mother goose
we forgot
to notice
all of life
is moving infinitely
slow
as the butterfly
reminds us

to enjoy the beauty
along the way
fast forward
on another day.

The Bank Account

how is it
that the bank account
is of no account
and by no means
a measure
of the treasure
within
however
when the zeros
start to multiply
at the end
a false sense of
security sets in
forgetting the true
treasure within.

Waiting in Line

the line forms in the rear
behind the man with the
baggy pants
he wants ice cream too
the line forms
in back of the mom
with three kids
waiting for water
the line forms
in back of the woman
with huge earrings
waiting to use the
restroom
lines in
the grocery store
weaving in and out
and all about

long lines
in the retail
outlets
and restaurants
just leave your name
and number
to be called
long lines at the ballet
and spiritual center too
I live in a place
where there is
no line at the bank
just float in and out
no line at the train station
or grocery store
no line to dine
no line to fine tune

yourself
just close your eyes
breathe and be.

The Overnight Guest

*the traveller
the ONE
that slips
ever so gently
into
the space
no one
would occupy
unless for the
occasional
overnight guest
the guest
can be
a stranger
a strange relative
of friend
slices of life*

are seen by
the overnight guest
opaque shadows
cast their shapes
around the
overnight guest
perched from the
circumference
the overnight guest
observes
witnesses
objectifies
the
comings and goings
settles in to pray
emit love
beam peace
radiate joy and move on.

The Push Cart

along the city streets
amid the noise and clamor
an oasis of delight appears
the push cart
overflowing with fruits
and veggies or gourmet treats
as well as exotic food from
foreign lands
the push cart
yogurt pops
nuts in honey
fancy crepes
plain old pretzels or a hot dog
all on the push cart
ever stop to wonder
how or where the
push cart goes
when day is done?

Vera Decicco

all that remains
is the faint
aroma of
the push cart.

Buy NOW

buy now
two words
in the little box
at the end of the line
BUY NOW
buy now
you need
this thing
no matter
the cost
sales are good
buy now
did the credit card
go through
buy now
need it or not
stop to think

is this flashing
buy now
so urgent
so necessary
so seductive
that it must be obtained
BUY NOW
turns into
BYE NOW
the choice
is yours
BYE NOW.

What Happened Today

what happened today
along the way
I happened today
happened to notice
the faces on the train
happened to hear
loving concern
on the phone
happened to feel
a touch of lightness
walking along the way
happened to remember
who I AM
I happened today
in a most amazing way.

Attachments

attachments
in an email
or a document
a vacuum cleaner
has attachments
a food processor
has attachments
certain addresses
or phone numbers
have attachments
the heart has
unseen attachments
a favorite song
a poem or a lost love
attachments
no wonder we carry our attachments
so secretly.

The New Normal

push the back button
to return to some kind
of normal
alas
the back button
does not carry us
back to normal
instead we are
fast forwarded
to the new
normal
which is
controlled craziness.

Mistaken Identity

and she slipped in the role
of mom
minister
friend
as if to change
shoes or hats
none of the above
to know the true self
the Self of self
she slips out of
mom
minister
friend
melts away
into the light
and just IS.

Attitude Adjustment

you say life stinks
so unfair
and upside down
or inside out
look again
look within
adjust the lens
see clearly
the beauty
in a flower
the joy in a child's laughter
the promise of spring
the awakening light
from within
look again
attitude adjustment.

Vera deCicco

Skinny Jeans

she went
from slim fit
to skinny jeans
in a flash
with legs
so tightly
bound and squeezed
like insect legs
supporting her frame
walking around
in a world of look alikes
all looking like insects
on stilts in
skinny jeans.

Change

change of season
change of heart
change in your pocket
change in the air
change erupting
change disrupting
change releasing
change moving
through stagnation
change emerging
and re arranging
into
NEW LIFE.

The Fitting Room

what a funny name
for a room
what is fitting and what
is not
the waist
the hips
the shoulders
the arms
and legs
or is it
fitting to sneeze
in one's face
or slurp soup loudly
or cut in front of someone
waiting in a long line
fitting or not
the room awaits.

Security

what is it
that gives a sense
of security
the full refrigerator
the bulging bank account
the guard in uniform at the door
or
could it be
as simple as
an apple
in the tote bag
as extra five bucks
or
overdraft protection
in the checking account
or
a hand to hold

while walking thru a rough patch
or
a welcoming
smile at the end of the day
or
a heated train station
whatever the level
of security
nothing compares
to the peace
of knowing
Divine Love
is our everlasting
security.

Travel Time

opening the door
stepping through
from one place
to another in
travel time
the Andes
the Himalayas
the Alps
the Rockies
travel time
the waterfalls
the rain forest
the volcanoes
travel time
oceans
islands
caves

Vera deCicco

deserts
the stars
the moon
the sun
the galaxy
in
travel time
stillness
abides.

Parts and Labor

we are made up
of many parts
and labor long
to know
how to
bring all of
those many parts
together
as one.

Vera deCicco

A Life of Glamor

she touched
a life of glamor
ever so lightly
through
galas
opera openings
ballet benefits
film premiers
gallery shows
broadway plays
all of this
to discover
a life of glamor
is to be enjoyed
ever so lightly
as it passes by.

The Universe Has Ears

did you ever stop to think
when uttering words or wishes
or just figures of speech
there is a big ear catching
all that floats around and
turns it into matter
as the vapors of a cloud
become rain or fog or snow
as a big red balloon
waiting to carry our words away
to return another day
in quite an unusual way
something to ponder or not.

Electronically Yours

it seem as if relationships
friendships
associates
etc. etc.
are surfacing ironically
electronically
via
facebook
twitter
text
or email
etc.
etc.
electronically yours
and so it goes
this sign off

greeting seems
most
appropriate
electronically yours.

Incidentals

overlooked
details
that silently
sit
along side
important
events
incidentals
signal
when
it's time
to pay mind
as in
running out
of toilet paper
when is the
last time
the rent
was paid

incidentals
where are
those earrings
did I forgive
myself for
being
unloving
uncaring
unaware
incidentals
coming into
oneness
within
the incidentals
melt and
matter not
in quiet
stillness.

Vera deCicco is a native New Yorker with a background in business as well as being an Interfaith Minister.

Her inspiration comes from the inner and outer landscapes of urban life. Seeing the beauty and irony both at once in everyday life, she writes poems of wit and wry as snapshots of the moment in passing.

Vera lives and works and has her being in Upper Manhattan.